OVERCOMING SHYNESS AND SOCIAL ANXIETY

Stop Feeling Insecure, Gain Confidence and Improve Your Social Life

Derek Sullivan

Uranus Publishing

ISBN 978-1-915218-11-7

Copyright © 2021 by Derek Sullivan - All rights reserved.

This book is copyright protected, and it is only for personal use. You cannot amend, distribute, sell, use, quote, or paraphrase any part of this book's content without the author or publisher's consent. All pictures contained in this book come from the author's archive or copyright-free stock websites.

Disclaimer Notice:

Please note the information contained within this document is for educational and entertainment purposes only. All effort has been executed to present accurate, up-to-date, reliable, complete information. No warranties of any kind are declared or implied. Readers acknowledge that the author is not engaged in rendering legal, financial, medical or professional advice. The content within this book has been derived from various sources. Please consult a licensed professional before attempting any techniques outlined in this book.

By reading this document, the reader agrees that under no circumstances is the author responsible for any losses, direct or indirect, that are incurred due to the use of the information contained within this document, including, but not limited to, errors, omissions, or inaccuracies.

The trademarks used are without any consent, and the publication of the trademark is without permission or backing by the trademark owner. All trademarks and brands within this book are for clarifying purposes only and are owned by the owners themselves, not affiliated with this document.

Contents

INTRODUCTION	1
1. THE SCIENCE BEHIND WHY SOME OF US ARE SHY	5
2. STRATEGIES TO OVERCOME SHYNESS	17
3. SHYNESS IN TEENAGERS	29
4. DEALING WITH LONELINESS AND SHYNESS	45
5. SOCIAL ANXIETY	57
6. INTROVERSION vs. SOCIAL ANXIETY	65
7. PUBLIC SPEAKING AND SOCIAL ANXIETY	75
8. SIMPLE STEPS TO FEELING MORE SOCIALLY CONFIDENT	85
9. SELF CONFIDENCE	93
10. HOW TO BE MORE SECURE WITH YOURSELF	109

CONCLUSION 127

130

INTRODUCTION

When you ask people what they are most afraid of, many of them will say "speaking in public." In surveys of individuals' concerns, around one out of every five persons has a severe dread of public speaking. Shyness and other forms of social anxiety are common, and they keep people from living their lives to the fullest.

Shyness is defined as a tendency to withdraw from others, particularly strangers. Everyone is bashful to some extent. In fact, a person who isn't shy is likely to make poor decisions when it comes to maintaining acceptable interpersonal boundaries.

A little shyness might be beneficial. However, when excessive shyness hinders a person from engaging in typical social interactions, performing effectively at work, or creating intimate relationships, it becomes a problem - one that may, thankfully, be overcome.

Shyness is a subset of social anxiety, which is a larger concept. This idea, sometimes known as social phobia, relates to a specific type of worry that people experience when close to others, and it's linked to apprehensions about being inspected. Although shyness and social anxiety are closely linked, social anxiety also encompasses events such as public speaking, taking tests, sports performance, and dating.

Embarrassment and shame are closely tied to the concepts of shyness and social anxiety. When something unexpected happens and draws unwelcome attention, a person experiences embarrassment (such as knocking over a glass of water in a restaurant). This causes a brief period of discomfort. Shame, on the other hand, has a longer lifespan. Shame is a negative emotion that arises when one is dissatisfied with oneself.

Who is most likely to be affected by social anxiety? Parents are aware that some children are easily terrified and cry a lot from birth, while others appear to be more resilient due to their temperament (they seldom cry, hardly ever get upset, and are less easily frightened).

Some kids are fascinated by the world around them, and others are wary of change and have a hard time with it. Inhibited children are more likely to have a parent who suffers from a social anxiety disorder. A person who is worried is more likely to have a parent or sibling who is depressed. Many patients with a social anxiety disorder say that one or both of their parents have a substance misuse problem, such as drinking, or that they come from a family that:

- There is a lot of tension amongst the adults.
- Parents are too judgmental of their children (nothing is ever good enough), and
- There is an overabundance of care for what other people think.

According to national studies, roughly 5% of children and adolescents suffer from a social anxiety disorder. Anxiety is rarely reported by children who have an anxiety disorder.

Instead, physical symptoms such as headaches, stomachaches, nausea, rapid heartbeat, dry mouth, flushing, dizziness, and shortness of breath are reported. Speaking in class, taking tests, reading aloud, writing on the board, inviting friends over to play, eating in front of others, going to parties, and participating in sports are all things they strive to avoid.

Social anxiety disorder in children and teenagers can lead to other issues such as loneliness, sadness, and low self-esteem. While some children will overcome their shyness over time as their fears fade away as they engage with others, others will see their symptoms grow. If a child's symptoms begin at the age of six and do not improve by the age of 10, it is time to seek expert help.

This book will teach you the principles, skills, and philosophy needed to break out and connect in a meaningful and comfortable way. Page after page, you will learn how to integrate yourself into other people's lives so that making friends and connecting with them becomes second nature.

Because I was shy for a period of time, I know it's doable. Now I'm liberated, connected, and content. I sincerely love myself and others. I feel that one of the key reasons for the high rate of suicide in the world today is loneliness. Putting these principles and talents into practice may not only free you, but also help others in a meaningful way.

To be very effective, you often only need good information and then to implement and practice what you've learned.

Chapter One

THE SCIENCE BEHIND WHY SOME OF US ARE SHY

When approaching or being approached by others, shyness is a feeling of embarrassment or apprehension that some people experience on a regular basis. Although shyness has neurobiology—the behavioral repertoire is coordinated by a specific circuit of neurons in the brain—research reveals that it is also substantially influenced by parenting techniques and life events.

Common questions about shyness

What are the reasons of shyness?

Self-consciousness, negative self-preoccupation, low self-esteem, and fear of judgment and rejection are all factors that contribute to shyness. Shy people frequently make exaggerated social comparisons, putting themselves against the most extroverted or enthusiastic people. Shy people avoid new social opportunities because they believe others are continuously judging them negatively, hindering them from strengthening their social abilities.

Are shy individuals born this way?

Excessive self-consciousness, negative self-evaluation, and negative self-preoccupation, all of which include a sense of self, characterize shyness. People cannot be born shy because their sense of self develops around the age of 18 months. Although 20% of children are born with a highly reactive temperament, this does not mean they will be shy or incapable of changing their behavior.

What causes youngsters to be shy?

Biological as well as environmental factors influence shyness. Babies are born with various temperaments, and those with a very sensitive temperament are more prone to become timid later in life. On the other hand, supportive, empathetic parenting can protect children from developing shyness or social anxiety.

What causes adolescent shyness?

Teenagers' shyness can be amplified during adolescence as they navigate new settings such as academics, friendships, and puberty. They may be afraid of being humiliated, rejected, or entirely exposed. Parents can encourage their children to consider how they would act if their worries were unfounded and then assist them in practicing such behaviors and abilities.

What's the difference between introversion and shyness?

Introversion is not the same as shyness. Time alone energizes introverts; shy people often want to connect with others but don't know how to handle the anxiety and dread of being judged negatively that comes with a human connection. Their propensity to look inward to assess their behavior and perceived flaws might make it difficult for them to form partnerships.

How does shyness differ by culture?

Children's social tendencies are influenced by the cultural values they learn from their parents and society. Around 40 to 50 percent of adults in the United States consider themselves shy, compared to

30 percent of Israelis and 60 percent of Japanese. These cultural variances are most likely due to differences in how people assign blame and praise.

Signs you are a shy person?

Are you one of those people who avoid conversing with strangers? Are you one of those persons who can't seem to get along with new people? Are you one of those persons that prefer to live alone and refuse to share things with others? If any of these apply to you, you are a shy person.

It's nearly impossible to talk to strangers

It's difficult for shy people to strike up a conversation with strangers. Shy people are unable to even greet strangers. I'm not sure why they have such a hard time doing it. Perhaps they are uncomfortable conversing with strangers. Don't worry, shyness isn't an illness.

We don't like to say anything unless we are at ease

When you first meet me, our discussion will be awkward regardless of what we talk about since I have no idea what to say. It's even worse if you're attractive. But if you give me a little time, I'll feel more at ease conversing with you. Then I'll start talking so loudly that you'll get annoyed. Shy people prefer not to communicate anything unless they feel at ease.

Lover's silence

The silent lovers are shy people who will never tell their sweetheart that they love them. But believe me when I say that shy people make the ideal lovers because their feelings for their spouse are sincere. Instead of proposing to their lover and being rejected, shy people prefer to be in silent love.

We don't hate anyone, but we're just used to our situation

Shy people are just at ease in their skin, but it doesn't mean we despise anyone. We're the kind of guys that don't get involved in other people's affairs; we just want to be alone. Whether you like us or not, you can't dispute that we're fantastic.

We may not be able to communicate, but we each see things in our way

This is our personality: we notice everything, yet they don't get noticed. We don't say anything; we don't say anything, but we see everything. Have faith in me. We are acutely aware of everything that is going on around us.

We are unable to mix with others

Shy people are closed off to a large number of people. Shy people are usually quiet and dislike being the center of attention. So if we talk to you and tell you our secret, you must be incredibly special. A shy person finds it difficult to make friends with new people, but if they do at first, it signifies you are really special to them.

The reasons behind people's shyness

What causes shyness, and why do shy people act in certain ways? Let's examine the psychology and causes of shyness.

So, what is it that makes people shy?

There is no single cause for shyness; rather, it results from a combination of events. A mix of nature and nurture can create shyness, and it can evolve as a person gets older and encounters new events.

Furthermore, people do not have to be shy for the rest of their lives; they might go through phases of shyness and moments in their lives when their self-confidence rises and falls.

Shyness can be caused by various factors, including harsh treatment, inaccurate self-perception, and difficult life transitions like divorce, a new job, or going away to school.

Causes of shyness at a young age

Even though there is no such thing as a "shy gene," children might begin to show signs of shyness as early as two. Babies may have a bashful demeanor that develops as they get older.

You must be aware of yourself in order to be shy. Because shyness is linked to self-consciousness, we typically associate it with children who can recognize themselves as separate individuals. A tendency to be shy from an early age, on the other hand, does not automatically imply that a person would live a life of social animosity. It also has a lot to do with a person's upbringing and experiences in life.

Shyness is frequently associated with fearing, according to popular opinion. Afraid children are far more likely than less fearful children to be timid.

Reasons of shyness in social situations

Shyness is commonly described as feeling uneasy in social circumstances, particularly when meeting new people. One of the main reasons why someone could feel uneasy in a social situation is that they are overly concerned with how their actions will be perceived. They are terrified of how others may react to them.

Shy people are more likely to focus on what they believe they are doing wrong, and they may allow previous negative experiences to influence current events. Shyness can be like a continual voice in a shy person's brain, advising them to fear new situations because they believe they will fail. Shy persons may also blame any perceived social failure on a personal flaw.

Shyness can also stem from a child's interaction with an anxious, rejecting, critical, or restricted parent (usually of the same sex).

According to research, shy and non-shy toddlers perceive emotion in different ways due to physiological and neurological variations. When shy children were shown video clips depicting fear and grief, EEG monitoring devices found that they had much greater brain activity in the right anterior portion of their brain than non-shy youngsters.

Shyness is a challenging state to observe in others, even more difficult to experience firsthand, and even more difficult to express.

How the wrong approach can increase a person's shyness

People who are not shy may be outspoken or even hostile toward people who are, which might exacerbate the situation. It could simply be an attempt to 'break through' the other person's shell. However, approaching someone who is shy in this manner is typically not the greatest method because it may draw unwanted attention to them, making them feel self-conscious and uncomfortable.

A more in-depth examination of the variables

Let's take a closer look at some of the most common ways that shyness develops in children.

- Inability to participate in social circumstances due to a lack of understanding

Children could be shy because they don't know how to act in particular social circumstances. As a result, when they are confronted with situations in which they are expected to express themselves or participate, they may flee in terror.

When you think about it, kids have a lot less life experience than adults do. Many of the situations that children face are unfamiliar to them, and they may lack the necessary abilities to deal with them. A child's anxiety of continuously having to react to new settings with unknown individuals may cause him or her to withdraw.

- There is far too much taunting and criticism

Children who are excessively teased, criticized excessively, and even threatened may develop a habit of receiving negative responses from others. It's no surprise, however, that their self-esteem may be severely harmed and that they may believe that everyone dislikes them. As a result, social events and contact with other people are avoided. On the other hand, children with low self-esteem expect others to feel the same way about them.

Parenting errors

- Parenting that isn't consistent

When a child is disciplined for a behavior one day and then receives no punishment the next, they are experiencing inconsistent parenting. Inconsistent parenting can make a youngster feel insecure, and they may believe their parent is overly involved at times and underly involved at others.

- Absence of participation

Parents may convey the impression to their children that they do not have the time or want to be involved in their child's life. This can be quite harmful to a child. If a parent shows uninterest in their child's growth, the child may withdraw from social situations, fearing that they will be viewed as worthless or "not worth it."

Overcoming shyness

Shy persons can successfully deal with social obstacles while maintaining their sense of self. According to researchers, it's often preferable for people to admit their shyness and try to let go of their self-consciousness.

A variety of concrete tactics can help people feel more confident in social situations. Instead of avoiding social situations, shy people should plan ahead of time and practice their social skills. They can prepare a few questions and talking points and monitor the discussion to get a sense of what's going on. They can also attempt to change their thinking by anticipating a positive outcome rather than assuming a unavoidable negative reaction.

How can I overcome my shyness?

When you're preparing for a social event, you might change your emphasis away from what could go wrong and toward what could go right. Prepare some questions for others and some anecdotes to offer. Consider what you may have in common. It can also be beneficial to be curious about others and to lessen your self-criticism.

Can I outgrow shyness?

Shyness does not go away by itself. Shy people are most effective when they recognize and understand their shyness, then act on that understanding. They understand that small conversation may not come readily to them, so they prepare ahead of time, practice questions and tales, and arrive early to feel at ease in the unfamiliar environment.

What can I do to encourage my child to be more outgoing?

Parents can assist shy children in making friends without forcing them to be someone they are not. Friendships can form around a shared activity, so parents can foster their children's interests. Basic social skills like making eye contact, smiling, speaking correctly, and asking "what" and "how" questions can also be taught.

Chapter Two

STRATEGIES TO OVERCOME SHYNESS

If you've struggled with shyness for a long time, you've probably heard of well-intentioned advice:

- "All you have to do is smile and say hi!" says the narrator.
- "All you have to do now is go talk to them." They're not going to bite."
- "Stop second-guessing anything."

Of course, this advice is frequently given by people who have little (if any) experience with shyness. Chronic shyness extends beyond the transitory emotions of unease and apprehension that most people feel in particular settings, such as their first day on the job.

In most social circumstances, shy people feel self-conscious and uncomfortable.

Perhaps the prospect of meeting new people makes you feel jittery, sweaty, and nauseated. You question that other people are interested in you, and you are concerned about what other people think of you throughout interactions.

In other words, shyness isn't something you can just mask with a grin. Shyness doesn't normally go away on its own, but the 12 tactics listed below can help you begin to feel more at ease around others and with yourself.

1. Look into possible sources

Experts agree that shyness develops as a result of a mix of variables, such as:

- life experiences
- genetics
- childhood environment

Shyness may be exacerbated by parental techniques, for example. In the event that your parents:

- Exaggerate potential hazards are d: You may have grown up approaching strangers and circumstances with tremendous care and reserve.
- Set severe limits on what you may and cannot do: Even as an adult, you can be hesitant to go beyond such boundaries.
- Were shy or anxious themselves: You most likely noticed this response and eventually began to imitate it.

Instability in your surroundings can also play a role, such as:

- having to relocate frequently
- dealing with bullying
- living in a dangerous neighborhood
- going through substantial family dynamics changes as a result of divorce or death

Any of these elements can influence how you deal with social situations.

Shyness can emerge at any age, including puberty and maturity. If your peers have rejected you or if your professors and supervisors have singled you out for criticism, it's reasonable to be fearful of similar humiliating situations in the future.

Discovering the source of your shyness might help you locate the correct tools to modify your fear.

2. Determine whether the problem is due to shyness or something else

Shyness, social anxiety, and introversion are frequently confused as synonyms.

Some shy people may be diagnosed with a social anxiety disorder (or introversion, or both). However, social anxiety is a mental illness, but shyness is not.

A continuous fear of rejection, disapproval, and criticism from others is what social anxiety is all about. This dread may become so intense that you avoid social situations totally.

If you're shy, you can feel awkward among new people at first, but as you get to know them better, you'll find it easier to interact. Shyness does not always result in the same level of distress as social anxiety.

It's also possible that others assume you're shy when you just want to be alone.

If you're introverted, you may not find it difficult to socialize — that is when you're in the mood to do so.

You don't shun other people because you're embarrassed or worried about what others think of you. You opt to spend time alone because you require isolation to function at your best.

3. Examine your assets

Consider shyness from an evolutionary standpoint for a moment.

You might have ventured out to explore new locations, find resources, and interact with other groups if you were outgoing. If you were shy, you might have kept close to home to avoid any danger.

Both responsibilities are required. However, while exploration may lead to fresh discoveries, it also places you in the line of potential perils. Staying in one location keeps you protected.

However, rather than viewing shyness as a defect, it can be beneficial to emphasize your talents. Recognizing the areas where your skills really shine can enhance your self-confidence, which can help reduce feelings of insecurity and self-doubt.

Perhaps you're a natural with animals, a gifted artist, or a dedicated scholar. Maybe you're a good listener, and your family and friends always come to you for advice.

The world requires equilibrium and what better way to attain that balance than through the use of many personality types?

Sure, it could take a little longer for you to open up. When you do, though, you have a lot to offer, such as empathy, sensitivity, and prudence.

4. Establish objectives

If you know someone who seems to make new acquaintances every time they enter a room, you might admire their outgoing personality and imagine yourself handling social situations with ease.

It's not impossible, but it's usually better to start with tiny steps.

Begin by examining the following aspects of your life that are impacted by shyness:

- "I'd like to be in a relationship, but I'm too timid about meeting people face to face."
- "My mark is based on my involvement in class, which accounts for 5% of my overall grade. But I'm afraid to tell anyone because I don't know anyone."
- "For this new project at work, I have a lot of ideas, but what if no one likes them?"

Then, utilizing that list, set simple goals for yourself, such as striking up a discussion with a classmate or using a dating app to identify suitable companions.

5. Don't be fooled by the lighting effect

In simple terms, the spotlight effect refers to the (often incorrect) belief that other people notice everything you do and say as if a spotlight were beaming on you.

This cognitive bias might exacerbate feelings of shyness or social anxiety.

When you're worried that others will notice and criticize your flaws, you're more prone to linger on the outskirts of a gathering, where you can protect yourself from possible rejection.

In actuality, most individuals are less observant than you might believe, partly because they're preoccupied with their own limelight. You may believe that all eyes are on you, but this is rarely the case.

Are you still not convinced? Consider how much you pay attention to the individuals you're around and what they're doing at any given time.

6. Take a more conscious approach to communications

Casual conversations can be nerve-wracking for timid people.

Even if you have a lot to say about a topic, concerns about how others in the conversation will view you may push those insights or humorous quips to the back of your mind.

You can wind yourself doing a lot of nodding or asking questions, so you don't have to say anything.

While asking questions can help people learn more about you, it does not help them come to know you. To put it another way, you're not truly connecting.

Investigate alternatives to asking a lot of questions to get to know someone.

Use active listening skills to focus on the flow of the discussion rather than pondering what they think of you or attempting to figure out what you should say.

Listening to what they're saying can help you break the cycle of fearing you'll sound awkward or say something embarrassing. You'll probably be able to recognize when it's more natural to express your opinions — and you won't be surprised when they ask you a question.

7. Be sincere

Some shy people use a confident façade to get through social situations.

However, "fake it 'til you make it" does not always succeed. Putting on a brave front when you don't feel it can make you even more worried that everyone will see right through you.

It's quite acceptable to state you're scared or to inform others that you want to ease into a group at your own pace. People may even express their gratitude for the effort you're putting in. And their affirming responses might genuinely boost your self-assurance.

Even if you think pretending would keep the conversation flowing, avoid white lies.

Telling your new housemates, "Yoga?" may appear to be perfectly innocuous. That's how I like to unwind." Consider how this could backfire. They might invite you to their Sunday yoga class when you've never done a Downward-Facing Dog before.

Tell the truth instead: "I've never done yoga but would like to!"

8. Recruit help

Support from someone you can trust can make you feel more at ease in the situations that cause you the greatest anxiety.

Of course, you can't have someone with you everywhere, but the goal is that you'll eventually feel prepared to confront those circumstances on your own.

Invite a friend, family member, or roommate to join you on your next social outing, whether it's a quiz night, a party, or a shopping excursion.

Their presence may provide enough security for you to navigate interactions without stumbling over your words or forgetting what you were going to say.

Some people find it beneficial to have some "practice" encounters with loved ones so that they may become accustomed to responding to positive, negative, and neutral input. Don't forget that interacting with family and friends might help you improve your communication abilities.

Ask a friend or family member to role-play scenarios that make you feel uneasy, such as being singled out for attention.

9. Appreciate the advantages of shyness

So, perhaps you have a hard time opening up to new people straight immediately, or you are nervous before speaking with someone new.

While this may mean you have a harder time making friends or finding dates than more extroverted people, it's worth remembering that a little caution never hurts.

When you meet new individuals, holding back provides you the opportunity to learn more about them before jumping into a friendship or relationship.

It also provides more room for trust to grow, which is always a good thing. After all, a delayed start frequently leads to deeper connections later on.

10. Accept yourself

Whatever caused your shyness, it's simply a part of your personality at this point. You can work on being less shy, but there's no need to push yourself to overcome it if your shyness isn't bothering you.

For example, you may not feel compelled to meet new people, but you have no trouble greeting someone when they are introduced to you. Even if your heart beats a little quicker before speaking with your boss, you handle talks successfully when they are required.

So you're not a big social butterfly. This is not the case for everyone!

If you're timid and introverted, you may be quite content with your current level of social involvement because it allows you to recharge and unwind on your own.

11. Keep in mind that avoidance isn't a viable option.

It can feel a lot safer to skip out on social occasions totally than to try and fail to make friends.

Avoiding people may insulate you from rejection, but it also increases your chances of loneliness. You'll have to find a way to connect with others if you want to broaden your social circle.

Exploring your passions — hiking, crafting, dancing, cooking, and so on — through classes, community activities, or even applications like Meetup might help you meet possible friends and companions who share your passions.

12. Consult a therapist

Shyness isn't a mental health issue in and of itself, but it can lead to emotional suffering over time. If nothing seems to help, you relax in social circumstances, consulting a professional might be a useful next step.

A therapist can assist you with:

- taking care of your physical symptoms
- investigating the reasons for shyness in greater depth
- recognizing social anxiety and other issues
- re-framing and addressing avoidance-inducing notions
- figuring out how to deal with social circumstances

When it comes to bodily symptoms, you can attempt some anxiety-relieving breathing or body movement exercises. Begin with these breathing techniques, which can help with any type of worry.

Chapter Three

SHYNESS IN TEENAGERS

It's difficult to approach adolescence without feeling bashful a lot of the time, and there is a slew of new situational annoyances.

For example, the consequences of puberty during early adolescence generate a vulnerability to being taunted about physical appearance, which might cause reluctance to socialize with classmates. Young people who "detest" how they appear can remain to themselves to avoid being scrutinized by others, whether by comparing themselves negatively or by just comparing themselves to others.

A sixth-grade girl or boy may dread dressing in public for physical education at school if she or he is uncomfortable with her or his bodily changes. Shyness is frequently caused by severe self-consciousness.

Shyness and self-consciousness

Furthermore, many adolescents are more reserved towards adults than children, as adults have become the de facto benchmark for behaving more maturely. It's now common to avoid adult companionship since one feels diminished and inhibited in their presence.

The only child who has been socialized to act adult by the companionship of parents is a common exception to adolescent shyness around adults. She feels herself to be on par with them and has been friends with their friends since she was a toddler. Growing up as an only child has many advantages, including social confidence in dealing with adults.

On the other hand, this familiarity with adults can occasionally lead to another source of shyness: feeling out of step with peers. "Adults are more accepting of me than my peers. Other kids don't understand my sense of humor as well as adults do."

Even late-adolescents are susceptible to timidity. Consider fresh college students who don't know anyone on campus and must attend parties in order to meet people. Many people use alcohol to self-medicate social anxiety and overcome uncomfortable shyness. They can become enough open and outgoing after drinking to make it through the evening, presumably without incident. Shyness is a common occurrence during adolescence.

Then there's temperamental shyness, which appears to combine a lack of self-confidence, inadequate conversational abilities, and social anxiety, all of which lead to the young person avoiding the social connection that he or she truly wants. Shyness can become its own worst enemy when a teenager's shyness causes them to act shy, which makes them feel even shyer.

Keeping others at a safe distance, remaining silent, not greeting others, murmuring when spoken to, avoiding eye contact, and choosing to sit alone all hinder the youngster from engaging in the social interactions that they fear and miss.

Then there's the possibility that others will misinterpret a shy person's actions as anti-social. A teenager determined to act more open in high school after making and keeping a "new school resolution" to break out from her past of bashful seclusion. She did so successfully, and she relayed what her new group of pals told her with amazement.

"Can you believe they thought I was a snob in middle school? They assumed I was keeping to myself because I was feeling superior to them! They mistook me for someone who didn't want anything to do with them while all I wanted was to be their buddy!" When you act timid, you can come out as uninterested, superior, or even anti-social.

Temperamental shyness

Temperamental shyness can be costly in adolescence when it becomes an impediment to social development. Consistently behaving shy in adolescence might have a negative impact on adult social skills. So, what can parents do if they notice their adolescent is becoming socially avoidant, distant, secluded, or even reclusive?

One of a parent's responsibilities is to plan forward for a teenager who is more focused on the present. As a result, they can respond, "We understand that being outgoing can be difficult for you, but making an effort to do so is worthwhile. In the years ahead, you'll need to know how to approach people, communicate with them, speak out for yourself, and socialize in groups of people."

Parents must be mindful of four prevalent worries that contribute to adolescent shyness when promoting this development.

There's a fear of being discovered. "I dislike being the center of attention. I'd rather just sit back and watch what's going on."

There's a dread of being humiliated. "I don't want to do or say anything dumb in front of other people. I'd prefer not to take part."

There is apprehension about being rejected. "I don't want to reach out only to be ignored or rejected. I'd want to be alone."

The fear of being mute exists. "I don't want to start speaking and then become speechless. I'd rather remain silent."

Overcoming fear is frequently required to recover from shyness. Parents should make it obvious that everyone experiences shyness at some point in their lives. In reality, they can describe how they felt through times of shyness, how they felt, and how they summoned the confidence to face their fears.

The difference between utilizing fear as an informant and as an advisor is crucial to assist the shy adolescent in making. Fear, as an informant, tells us that we are in danger, which is useful information to have. On the other hand, fear can advise us to avoid, flee, or hide, all of which can make us much more terrified.

Parenting the shy teenager

To overcome shyness, you must have the guts to make counterintuitive decisions. Despite our dread, we must choose to act in a non-fearful, confident, and outgoing manner.

Parents must respect the ambivalence of the adolescent who wants to break free from the prison of shyness but is afraid of leaving the safety of that haven. They can then give some basic directions.

"The ability to act less shy begins with a desire to be more socially comfortable. The next step is to get the guts to practice becoming more outgoing. This necessitates posing and answering the freedom question: 'How would I act in social situations if I wasn't shy?' Now write out all of the physical, communicative, responsive, assertive, and friendly behaviors you would exhibit if you weren't fearful. These are some of the skills you'll need to master. The more you practice them, the less awkward and accustomed they will become, the greater social connection you will have with people as they connect with you, and the less shyness will get in your way. Courage will lead to confidence, practice will lead to proficiency, and positive feedback from others will validate your efforts."

Telling shy teenagers that chatting together is simply one technique to create social interactions is one strategy for helping them overcome their worries of speaking up and engaging in conversation. Another thing to do is to do it jointly. Companionship is formed in both directions.

Encourage timid adolescents who don't know what to say or don't have anything to say to join a common-interest group where everyone already has something they enjoy doing and where the focus is on doing it when they get together.

The shy adolescent now has an advantage in social situations. He enjoys and is knowledgeable about what others enjoy and are knowledgeable about.

He can start playing and interacting with them right away. And he realizes that he has a lot to say to those who are interested in the same topics. I've seen youngsters begin to overcome their shyness by joining a number of common-interest groups, such as a sports team, a fantasy gaming team, a movie-making team, a volunteer club, or a theater troupe, to name a few.

Of course, the Internet has been both a benefit and a curse when it comes to shyness. It's been a boon because a timid person who feels mute in person can discover words by typing out what he or she wants to express, acquiring confidence in verbal fluency in the process. This is also one of the reasons why texting is so popular: you don't have to be seen or heard to communicate, and it's almost instantaneous.

The drawback is that this method only gets you so far. There is no substitute for face-to-face, eye-to-eye, spoken conversation, in which knowing each other is informed by all of the non-verbal indications each person is giving and picking up.

This is full, not limited, exposure communication. This is unscripted conversation, not carefully rehearsed communication. There is nowhere to hide in this type of communication. A young person who conducts almost all of their online relationships may avoid direct, unmediated interactions with others. They can build social disability by avoiding social unpleasantness.

A young man once characterized shyness to me with a phrase that stuck with me: "When you're shy, you're there, but you're really not there."

"Do you mean like this?" I also recounted an ancient children's rhyme: "I met a man who wasn't there yesterday on a stairwell. I ran into him again today. I'd like for that man to leave!"

He replied, "Yes." "Shyness is the man that everyone wishes would vanish."

Five ways to shake shyness

A shy personality isn't always a bad thing. It's completely acceptable to take your time acclimating to new people and settings. However, shyness prevents some people from feeling as at ease or gregarious as they would like.

Some people wish to be less timid to enjoy mingling and being themselves in front of others. Here are some suggestions for overcoming shyness:

Begin with folks you already know. With the people you feel most comfortable around, practice social skills like eye contact, confident body language, introductions, small talk, asking questions, and invites. Smile. This is a great method to boost your self-assurance. Then venture out and do it with new people.

Make a list of discussion starters. Getting started with a new person is often the most difficult aspect. Introduce yourself ("Hi, my name is Chris, and we're in the same English class"), provide a compliment ("That jacket looks excellent on you"), or ask a question ("Do you know when our report is due?"). It's easier to approach someone if you have a conversation opener (or several).

Make a list of what you want to say and practice saying it. Write down what you want to say beforehand when you're ready to do something new that you've been putting off due to your shyness, such as a phone call or a discussion. Rehearse it aloud, if possible in front of a mirror. Then go ahead and do it.

Don't be concerned if it isn't exactly as you practiced or if it isn't flawless. Few of the things that more self-assured people appear to accomplish are perfect. Be pleased of yourself for giving it a shot. It'll be even better next time because it'll be easier.

Give yourself a chance to succeed. Look for group activities where you may spend time with people who have similar interests to you. Allow yourself the opportunity to practice socializing with these new people and progressively get to know them.

Shy people are frequently concerned about failing or being judged negatively by others. These kinds of concerns and thoughts can deter you from attempting. If you're prone to self-criticism, consider if you'd be as harsh on your best buddy.

You'd probably be a lot more welcoming. As a result, treat yourself as though you were your own closest friend. Instead of expecting to fail, encourage yourself.

Assertiveness is something you should work on. Because shy people are often overly concerned with the reactions of others, they don't want to upset the balance. That doesn't make them cowards or wimps.

However, it may indicate that they are less forceful. Assertiveness entails standing up for yourself when necessary, asking for what you want or need, and letting others know when they're stomping on your toes.

Above everything, stay true to yourself. It's fine to experiment with different conversational strategies you've seen others use. However, say and do what suits your personality. Friends are drawn to people who are themselves — and who are willing to let themselves be acknowledged.

Teen therapy and self-esteem

Shyness can cause a range of issues for children, including falling behind in school because they are afraid to approach the teacher and ask questions. When a timid child learns to overcome these issues, they can gain long-term rewards.

Teaching kids to think more favorably about themselves is a big part of boosting their self-esteem. Teen therapy accomplishes this in a variety of ways, including:

1. Reducing self-blame, humiliation, and negative thoughts

Your teen will have more time to get to know themselves with the help of a qualified therapist. They'll teach them how to recognize negative self-talk, the events that lead to these beliefs, and how to deal with them. Your teen can then learn strategies to help them enhance their self-esteem.

2. Developing empathy for oneself

Developing self-compassion is one way to improve their self-esteem. The therapist can guide them to treat themselves with the same kindness they show to others. Self-empathy allows your kid to obtain a deeper understanding of themselves and the challenges they're dealing with by unlocking it.

3. Developing positive mental patterns and outlooks

A therapist will teach your teen how to turn negative self-talk into positive affirmations about themselves, in addition to countering bad beliefs. Empowering your kid to create good adjustments in their mental patterns will help them feel comfortable with and enjoy their own feelings and thoughts.

4. Developing social skills and behavioral habits that are effective

A therapist will urge your teen to participate in activities that will help them interact with their peers while also increasing their confidence and competence. It's critical to put new abilities and behavioral patterns into practice, not just with the therapist's help but also with their parents'.

5. Developing a sense of achievement

Your teen will get a stronger sense of self, and a sense of success in what they can achieve as the therapist assists them in not just accepting their weaknesses but also seeing their genuine strengths. Receiving praise from others, such as the therapist and their parents, will allow kids to appreciate their accomplishments. They learn to be proud of who they are as a result.

Some of the techniques utilized in teen counseling

Exposure Therapy

The adolescent will eventually be exposed to situations that he or she fears. The least frightening ones come first, followed by increasingly challenging ones as they progress through each level. Social skill training, rehearsal, and practice in real-life circumstances are all part of exposure therapy.

CBT (Cognitive-Behavioral Therapy)

Adolescent learns to evaluate their thinking patterns in fearful situations and to replace negative thoughts with good ones. They try acting out particular circumstances with their therapist or other group members, armed with their new thoughts. Then, individuals are encouraged to address these difficulties in real-life situations by utilizing their newly acquired coping strategies.

Relaxation training may be included in CBT to assist patients to learn to stay calm when presented with fearful events. To learn more about teen counseling, go here.

How can parents assist their shy teenagers?

You probably want to know what you can do as a parent to help your teen. If your teen is suffering from a social anxiety disorder, therapy is a good place to start. You can also help your teen by doing the following:

1. Validate your feelings and express compassion

Recognize that your teen may be experiencing anxiousness. It's not something they feel they have control over as a parent and shy kid without treatment. Your adolescent may also be dealing with self-critical or negative ideas. Try not to dismiss or condemn their symptoms or behavior.

2. Encourage your youngster to conquer their concerns and join in the activity

Anxiety and avoidance behavior grow as a result of avoidance. Instead, encourage your youngster to think about solutions to problems and strategies to deal with difficult situations.

Help your teen understand their concerns and coping techniques if they wish to avoid a situation. "What are you terrified of?" Do you get irritated when you're singled out? Are you concerned about how the other children will perceive you?" "What's the worst that could happen (not in a sarcastic sense, of course!)" asks the question.

Then there's the question of "how likely is it that this will happen?" Assist them in moving towards their fears rather than away from them. Instead of avoiding school and social gatherings, encourage engagement.

3. Assist your shy adolescent in recognizing negative or perfectionistic beliefs and thoughts

Let your teen know that we all have unrealistic expectations of ourselves. There are various perspectives on a topic, and it's easy to select the negative one and follow it, even if it's unreasonable or doubtful. Encourage your teen to recast his or her views and expectations more realistically.

4. Hire a coach

Parents can benefit from learning strategies to cope with negative thoughts and beliefs for themselves and then teaching their kids how to use these tools.

Chapter Four

DEALING WITH LONELINESS AND SHYNESS

We're designed to be social beings as humans. We are happier and healthier when we have friends; being socially linked is essential for our mental and emotional well-being.

Many of us, on the other hand, are shy and socially introverted. We feel uncomfortable with strangers, unsure of what to say or concerned about what others may think of us. This might lead us to avoid social settings, isolate ourselves from others, and be isolated and lonely.

Loneliness is a problem that affects people of all ages and backgrounds, yet most of us are reluctant to confess it. However, loneliness is not anything to be embarrassed about. It can also be the result of external conditions, such as moving to a new area. You may do several things in these situations to meet new people and turn acquaintances into friends.

But what if you're shy, socially insecure, or have had a long-standing problem making friends? The truth is that none of us are born with the ability to interact with others. They're things we pick up through time, and the good news is that you can pick them up as well.

You may learn to silence self-critical thoughts, increase your self-esteem, and become more confident in your interactions with others, no matter how uneasy you are in the presence of others. You don't have to change your personality, but you can overcome shyness or social awkwardness, banish loneliness, and enjoy strong, fulfilling friendships by learning new skills and adopting a different viewpoint.

Taking on social anxiety and fear

The things we tell ourselves make a tremendous difference when it comes to shyness and social discomfort. Here are a few frequent thinking patterns that can erode your self-esteem and drive social anxiety:

- Believing you're dull, unlikable, or strange.
- In social situations, believing that others are analyzing and judging you.
- Believing that if you make a social error, you will be shunned and chastised.
- Believing that being rejected or socially shamed would be a terrible and life-changing experience.
- Believing that your identity is defined by what others think of you.

It's no surprise that social situations appear intimidating if you believe these things! The truth, on the other hand, is rarely so black-and-white.

People aren't thinking about you to the extent that you believe. The majority of people are preoccupied with their own lives and problems. Other individuals are thinking about themselves, just as you are thinking about yourself and your societal problems. Stop wasting time worrying about what others think of you because they don't spend their free time judging you.

Many other people are just as nervous and awkward as you are. When you're socially nervous, it can feel as if everyone else is an outgoing, self-assured extrovert. That, however, is not the case. Some people are better at disguising it than others, but there are a lot of introverts out there that have the same self-doubts you do. The next person you speak with is just as concerned about your opinion of them!

People are more tolerant than you may believe. The thought of doing or saying anything embarrassing in public is terrifying to you. You're certain that everyone will pass judgment on you. In reality, though, people are unlikely to make a huge deal out of a social faux pas. Because everyone has done it at some point, most people will simply dismiss it and move on.

Accepting yourself is a skill

You'll feel less apprehensive in social situations once you realize that others aren't scrutinizing and condemning your every word and deed. But there's still the issue of how you feel about yourself. We're typically our own harshest critics. We're harsh on ourselves in ways we'd never be harsh on strangers, let alone those we love.

It takes time to learn to embrace yourself; it necessitates a shift of mindset.

To be liked, you don't have to be flawless. In reality, our flaws and peculiarities can be endearing. Even our flaws might help us connect with others. It's a connecting experience when someone is honest and open about their flaws, especially if they can laugh at themselves. If you can accept your clumsiness and flaws with a smile, you'll discover that others will as well. They might even like you more as a result!

It's quite acceptable to make mistakes. Everyone makes errors; it's a natural part of life. So, if you make a mistake, give yourself a break. Being perfect does not increase your worth. If self-compassion is difficult for you, consider viewing your faults through the eyes of a friend. What would you say to your pal? Now it's time for you to take your own advice.

Your negative self-evaluations may or may not be accurate. They most likely don't, especially if you:

- Call yourself derogatory terms like "pathetic," "worthless," "dumb," and so on.
- Make a list of everything you "should" or "shouldn't" have done.
- Make broad generalizations based on a single occurrence. If something doesn't go as planned, you may persuade yourself that you'll never do it right, that you're a failure, or that you always make mistakes.

It's critical to pause and intentionally dispute such mistaken thoughts when they arise. Pretend you're a neutral third-party observer, and then consider whether there are any alternate perspectives on the situation.

One step at a time, developing social skills

It takes work to improve social skills. Don't expect to get comfortable socially without putting in the time, just as you wouldn't expect to become competent at the guitar without putting in the time. You can, however, start small. Take small efforts toward being more self-assured and social, then build on your achievements.

- When you pass someone on the street, give them a friendly smile.
- Compliment someone you meet throughout the day.
- Ask someone a casual question (for example, "Have you been here before?" in a restaurant). "How's the steak coming along?")
- Introduce yourself to a pleasant cashier, receptionist, waiter, or salesperson.

How to confront your biggest social phobias

When it comes to the things that truly terrify us, we should approach our anxieties gradually, beginning with somewhat stressful situations and progressing to more anxiety-inducing events. Consider it a stepladder, with each rung a little more demanding than the one before it. Before moving on to the following phase, make sure you've had a good experience with the one before it.

If meeting new people at parties, for example, makes you nervous, here's a stepladder you may use:

- Attend a gathering and give a few folks a friendly grin.
- Ask a basic inquiry during a party (e.g., "Do you know what time it is?"). Once they've responded,

thank them cordially and then excuse yourself. The idea is to keep the interaction brief and to the point.

- Request that a friend introduce you to someone at the party to have a brief talk.
- Choose a partygoer who appears friendly and approachable. Please begin by introducing yourself.
- Approach a group of folks who aren't frightened at the party. You are not required to make a grand entrance. Simply join the group and listen in on the discussion. If you want to make a comment or two, go ahead and do so, but don't put too much pressure on yourself.
- Join another kind and approachable group. Try to participate in the discourse a little more this time.

More social-confidence-building advice

- Make it up as you go along. Acting self-assured might help you feel more self-assured.
- Concentrate on the outside world rather than on yourself. Switch your emphasis from yourself to the other person instead of thinking about how you're coming across or what you're going to say. You'll be more present in the moment and less self-conscious.
- Make a fool of yourself. Use humor to put things in perspective if you do something embarrassing. Laugh, learn and keep moving forward.
- Make an effort to assist others or to brighten someone's day. It could be as simple as a

compliment or a grin. You will feel better about yourself if you distribute positivity.

How to start a conversation

Some folks seem to know how to strike up a conversation with anyone in any situation. If you're not one of the lucky ones, these pointers will help you strike up a conversation when you meet someone new:

Remark on the environment or the occasion. For example, if you're at a party, you could make a favorable comment about the venue, the catering, or the music. "I adore this music," says the listener. "The cuisine is fantastic. "Have you tried the chicken?" says the narrator.

Ask an open-ended inquiry, one that doesn't demand a simple yes or no response. Ask a question that begins with one of the 5 W's (or 1 H): who, where, when, what, why, or how, as per the journalist's credo. "Who do you know here?" for example. "On Fridays, where do you usually go?" "How long have you been here?" "How do you keep yourself occupied?" "How did you decide to become a vegetarian?" "How's the wine?" says the narrator. Asking a question is a wonderful method to start a discussion because most individuals enjoy talking about themselves.

Make use of compliments. "I truly like your pocketbook; may I inquire as to where you acquired it?" for example. or "You appear to have done this before; could you please tell me where I need to sign in?"

Make a note of whatever you have in common and follow up with a question. "I also enjoy golf; what is your favorite local course?" "I attended that school with my daughter; how does your son like it?"

Small talk is a great way to keep the discussion going. Don't say anything overtly controversial, and steer clear of heavy topics like politics or religion. Stick on light topics like the weather, the environment, and anything you share in common, like school, movies, or sports teams.

Listen carefully. Waiting for your turn to speak is not the same as listening. You can't concentrate on what someone else is saying while planning what you'll say next. One of the keys to effective communication is to give your entire attention to the speaker and indicate that you are interested in what they are saying. Nod occasionally, smile at the person and maintain an open and inviting stance. Use modest verbal cues like "yeah" or "uh-huh" to encourage the speaker to continue.

What to do when you're tired of social situations

Introverts are often misunderstood to be socially inept. Introverts can, in fact, be just as social as extroverts. Introverts lose energy when they're near other people and recharge by spending time alone, whereas extroverts gain energy when they're around other people.

This means that even the most socially confident introverts will become exhausted after a long period of socializing. It doesn't imply that there's something wrong with you or that you can't have a satisfying social life. You simply need to be aware of your limitations and plan accordingly.

Don't overcommit. It's fine to decline social invites if you need a break or want to take a rest after socializing. For example, you may need to spend Sunday alone to recuperate and recharge after a wonderful Saturday out with friends.

Take short pauses. There will be times when you're exhausted, yet you won't be able to leave the situation for an extended period of time alone. Perhaps you're at a hectic business convention, on a weekend getaway with pals, or spending the holidays with family. In these situations, try to sneak away to a quiet place when it isn't considered impolite. Even a few minutes every now and again can have a significant effect.

Discuss your need for alone time with your family and friends. Recognize that socializing depletes your energy. It's nothing to be ashamed of, and hiding it will just make you more socially exhausted. Friends who care about you will be compassionate and willing to help you.

Dealing with rejection and social difficulties

There will be instances when you feel judged or rejected as you put yourself out there socially. You might have reached out to someone, but they didn't appear interested in conversing or forming a friendship with you.

There's no denying that rejection is unpleasant. It's vital to remember, though, that it's a natural part of life. Not everyone you approach will be eager to strike up a discussion, much less become friends. Meeting new people, like dating, invariably involves some level of rejection. The following suggestions will assist you in dealing with social setbacks:

Make an effort not to take things too seriously. The other person could be having a poor day, be preoccupied with other issues, or simply not be in the mood to communicate. Always keep in mind that rejection is as much about the other person as it is about you.

Keep everything in context. Someone else's opinion does not define you, and it does not rule out the possibility of making new friends. Take what you've learned and tried again.

Don't obsess over your blunders. Even if you say something you later regret, the other person is unlikely to recall it after a short period of time. Keep a positive attitude; don't call yourself a failure or tell yourself you'll never be able to make friends. Even the shyest people do it, and you will as well.

Chapter Five

SOCIAL ANXIETY

Social anxiety disorder, formerly known as social phobia, is an anxiety condition characterized by extreme self-consciousness and overwhelming anxiety in everyday social situations.

Overview and more

People with social anxiety disorder are terrified of being watched and judged by others and being embarrassed or humiliated by their own actions.

Their dread may be so intense that it interferes with their ability to work, go to school, or participate in other activities.

Many persons who suffer from social anxiety disorder are aware that their fear of being among people is excessive or illogical, but they cannot overcome it. They frequently stress for days or weeks before a dreadful circumstance occurs. They also frequently suffer from low self-esteem and despair.

Social anxiety disorder might be restricted to a certain situation—for example, a fear of public speaking—or it can manifest itself whenever a person is in the company of others. Social phobia can have serious repercussions if left untreated. It may, for example, impede people from going to job or school or from making friends.

Blushing, sweating, trembling, nausea, and difficulty speaking are among physical symptoms that typically accompany the high stress of social anxiety disorder. Because these visual signs heighten the fear of rejection, they can become a source of fear in and of themselves, producing a vicious cycle: The more persons with social anxiety disorder worry about getting these symptoms, the more likely they are to do so.

Anxiety disorders such as panic disorder and obsessive-compulsive disorder are common in families and might be accompanied by depression or other anxiety disorders. Self-medicating with alcohol or other medications can lead to addiction in people with social anxiety disorder.

Within 12 months, about 7% of the US population is considered to have a social anxiety disorder. Social anxiety disorder affects roughly twice as many women as it does males, even though men seek treatment for it at a higher rate. The illness usually manifests itself in childhood or early adolescence, and it seldom manifests itself after the age of 25.

Symptoms

Only if the avoidance, fear, or anxious anticipation of a social or performance setting interferes with daily routine, occupational functioning, or social life, or if the anxiety causes significant distress, is a diagnosis of social anxiety disorder made.

The following criteria are listed in the DSM-5 for diagnosing social anxiety disorder:

• The person is afraid of one or more social or performance circumstances in which others may scrutinize him or her. Meeting new people, being seen eating or drinking, or giving a speech or performance are all examples.
• The person is afraid of causing shame or being harshly judged if they act inappropriately.
• Social circumstances almost always induce a great deal of anxiety.

- The dreaded scenario is avoided or endured with dread and worry.
- The fear or anxiety is out of proportion to the social situation's actual threat.
- The fear or anxiety is long-lasting, usually lasting six months or more.
- The person's social, intellectual, or occupational functioning is considerably hampered by avoidance, nervous anticipation, or distress.

The following are some of the physical signs of social anxiety disorder:

- Blushing, sweating, trembling, a racing heart, or the sensation of your mind "going blank" are all symptoms of anxiety.
- Nausea or a stomachache
- Having a stiff body posture, failing to make eye contact, or speaking too quietly
- Furthermore, the diagnostic can indicate whether the anxiety or fear is exclusively present while speaking or acting in front of an audience.

Causes

While research into the reasons for social anxiety disorder is still underway, several studies point to the amygdala, a tiny region in the brain. The amygdala is thought to be a major brain structure that regulates fear reactions.

It is possible to pass on social anxiety disorder to your children. First-degree relatives, on the other hand, have a two to six times higher risk of developing a social anxiety disorder. The National Institute of Mental Health (NIMH)-funded study also discovered the location of a gene in mice that impacts learned fearfulness.

Scientists are looking into the possibility that increased sensitivity to disapproval is physiological or hormonal in nature. Other academics are looking into the impact of the environment on the development of social phobia. Social anxiety disorder is linked to childhood maltreatment and trauma.

Treatment

A qualified mental health care provider can successfully treat the majority of anxiety disorders. Psychotherapy and medicines are frequently used to treat social anxiety disorder successfully.

Therapy

CBT (cognitive-behavioral therapy) is a type of psychotherapy that has been shown to be particularly successful in treating severe social anxiety.

One of the main goals of CBT and behavioral therapy is to lessen anxiety by removing beliefs or behaviors that contribute to the anxiety disorder's maintenance. Avoiding a feared thing or situation, for example, inhibits a person from learning that it is harmless.

Exposure is an important component of CBT for anxiety, in which clients address their fears. In most cases, there are three stages to the exposure process. The feared situation is first shown to the individual.

The second phase is to raise the likelihood of rejection in that setting to gain confidence in his or her ability to deal with rejection or criticism.

The third phase entails training someone on how to deal with disapproval. People are encouraged to envision their biggest fear and create positive reactions to this anxiety and perceived rejection at this stage.

These stages are sometimes accompanied by anxiety management training, such as teaching people how to control their anxiety through techniques like deep breathing. It may be feasible to defuse the anxiety associated with feared circumstances if done carefully and with the help of a therapist.

Exposure will be carried out only when you are ready; it will be done gradually and only with your permission if you are doing CBT or behavioral treatment. You'll work with your therapist to figure out how much you can manage and how quickly you can progress.

CBT and behavioral therapy have no negative side effects other than the momentary discomfort of heightened anxiety, but for the treatment to operate as intended, the therapist must be well-trained in the treatment techniques.

The therapist will most likely give homework during treatment—specific difficulties that the patient will need to work on in between sessions. CBT, or cognitive behavioral therapy, usually lasts 12 weeks. It can be done in a group if the members in the group have sufficiently similar difficulties.

Supportive therapy, such as group, couples, or family therapy, can inform loved ones about the disease. People who suffer from social anxiety may benefit from social competence training.

Medications

Along with psychotherapy, proper and effective drugs may play a part in treatment. Antidepressants such as selective serotonin reuptake inhibitors (SSRIs) and monoamine oxidase inhibitors (MAOIs), as well as high-potency benzodiazepines, are among the medications available.

Beta-blockers, which lower heart rate and diminish physical sensations of anxiety, have helped some people with a type of social anxiety that only appears when they have to perform in front of others.

It's critical to realize that treatments for social anxiety disorder don't work right away and that no single strategy works for everyone. Each person's treatment must be adjusted to their own needs.

A therapist and patient should collaborate to design the most effective treatment plan and to review whether the treatment plan appears to be on track. Because patients respond to treatment differently, it is occasionally necessary to make changes to the plan.

Chapter Six

INTROVERSION vs. SOCIAL ANXIETY

You have a narrow social circle and guard your alone time with your life. It takes some time until you feel comfortable opening up in front of strangers. You hold back and don't speak out unless it's absolutely necessary at work or school.

Parties and large groups of people make you feel uneasy, if not completely overwhelmed. You've turned to cancel plans into a fine art form. Others might describe you as restrained, quiet, or shy.

Do the traits listed above perfectly describe you? If that's the case, you're most likely an introvert.

Perhaps you've also considered whether something else is to blame for your lack of interest in social situations. You might question if your personality merely leans toward the introverted end of the spectrum, or if you have social anxiety.

The solution is contingent on two factors:

- the reasons why you find these practices to be the most natural
- how you feel about spending time with yourself

What's the difference?

Social anxiety and introversion can appear to be very similar on the surface. After all, they share a lot of the same symbols.

However, these two encounters are not identical, and they have less in common than you may expect.

Introversion

There is one important distinction between introversion and social anxiety: introversion is a personality trait, not a mental illness.

Introverted individuals get their energy from within. If you're an introvert, you probably spend a lot of your time alone. You enjoy relaxing and unwinding by yourself, so you may prefer to make plans with yourself rather than with others.

If you're an introvert, you can find yourself in the following situations:

- have excellent listening abilities
- before making a decision, think about all of your possibilities.
- aversion to conflict
- desire to express their emotions and ideas through writing or art

Because introversion is a personality feature, it is a natural part of who you are and not something you can change. Learning and honing certain skills can help you feel more at ease in a group setting, but they won't change how you acquire your energy.

Anxiety in social situations

If you have social anxiety, also known as social phobia, you are likely to feel uneasy and fearful in social situations or while just thinking about them. This worry usually arises from the fear that you will be rejected or judged harshly by others.

If you're introverted, you might prefer alone and stay to yourself. On the other hand, when you have social anxiety, you may desire to join the mob but are afraid of how you will be received – and possibly rejected.

When you go to parties or hang out with friends, you may find yourself spending a lot of time reflecting on what you've said or done and worrying about what others think of you.

You may experience the following symptoms as a result of social anxiety:

- I'm always afraid of doing anything embarrassing in public.
- Avoid communicating with persons you are unfamiliar with.
- Fixate on the prospect of social gaffes, such as forgetting someone's name or sneezing in the middle of a lecture.
- You're frustrated or lonely because you can't seem to connect with others the way you want to.

Because social anxiety is a mental health condition, the concern and fear you're experiencing may not go away without the help of a mental health expert.

Can you be a socially anxious introvert?

Introversion simply implies that you are fatigued by too much social engagement and need to recharge your batteries by spending time alone.

Introversion does not inevitably translate to social anxiety, and feeling drained by social interaction is not the same as feeling apprehensive about it.

You might be alright spending time with others as an introvert if you have enough energy, can leave anytime you need to, and the environment isn't too crowded or overpowering.

But what if you don't just require some alone time? What if you prefer your own company because you're constantly concerned about how others see you?

Perhaps one of the following scenarios is familiar to you:

- When you don't hear back from a buddy straight away, you start to worry that you've irritated them and go over your previous contacts with them.
- You sit silently in the back corner of meetings at work, hoping to go unnoticed. Your heart races, your palms sweat, and you're certain that everyone can see your hot face.

Keep in mind that introversion and its opposite, extroversion, are two sides of the same coin. You may fall closer to one end of the spectrum as an introvert, but it doesn't imply you shun people totally. Most introverts like spending time with their friends, especially those who respect their social limits and desire for alone time.

When avoidance and fear play a role in the amount of time you spend alone, it's worth considering whether social anxiety is a component.

While evidence suggests that introverts are more likely to have social anxiety, there is still a lot of variation in individual personality traits.

If you're more conscientious, you could worry about forgetting essential things or creating the appearance that you're untrustworthy.

If you have a high level of neuroticism, you may be more prone to feelings of uneasiness, stress, and anxiety when confronted with unfamiliar situations.

In addition, if you are more on the outgoing end of the scale, you may have social anxiety. To put it another way, you can be a "anxious extrovert" if you want to be.

What role does shyness play?

Shyness is a personality trait that is frequently confused with social anxiety and introversion. It's even been stated that social anxiety is just a severe case of shyness.

Like people with social anxiety, Shy people are often uneasy around strangers and hesitant to open out in social circumstances.

If you're a shy person, you could:

- In social situations, prefer to converse via text or email and keep close to good pals.

- Before speaking in front of a group, you flush, sweat, or feel ill to your stomach because you're nervous about meeting new people and wondering if they'll like you.

However, shyness often fades as you gain confidence. You might, for example, have no qualms about stating your thoughts in front of close friends. Similarly, if you feel liked and accepted at a party, your nerves may begin to fade.

It's difficult to discern where one stops and the other begins when social anxiety, introversion, and shyness coexist. Many people, however, are shy or introverted without also having social anxiety.

In reality, older research reveals that while shy people are more likely to suffer social anxiety, many shy people do not endure the long-term distress that comes with it.

Is it possible for them to influence each other?

If you're shy, introverted, and have social anxiety, the three factors can compound, making social encounters even more daunting to comprehend.

The birthday celebration for your dearest pal is approaching. They've organized a smaller, more intimate evening of board games and snacks, and you know they really want you to come.

However, you are aware that they have brought a few fresh acquaintances, most of whom you are unfamiliar with. You're nervous about playing your favorite games in a new environment.

Introversion may urge you to schedule a night for yourself before and after the party to prepare.

If you're shy, you could be concerned about meeting new people, but remember that your friend will be there to encourage you.

Adding social anxiety to the mix might make matters much more complicated.

What if you don't know how to play the game or forget a rule, you might wonder? What if you spill your drink all over the table, completely ruining everyone's night? What if you tell a joke and no one, including your best friend, laughs?

These concerns consume your thoughts in the days preceding up to the party until you're nauseous, scared, and ready to cancel and spend the evening alone.

When is it OK to contact someone?

Friendships and partnerships can be tough to pursue when you have social anxiety.

While you wish to participate more completely in social situations, your concerns of rejection and criticism keep you from making the connections you want.

You could:

- long to make friends and feel more comfortable in the company of others
- feel worse, not better, after spending time alone
- spend a lot of time worrying about negative feedback or judgment
- use alcohol to help manage your fears
- have trouble participating in daily interactions at school or work

Social anxiety can lead to feelings of isolation, loneliness, and even depression over time. A therapist's help, on the other hand, can make a tremendous difference.

A therapist can help you with:

- provide assistance in overcoming anxieties of rejection and judgment give skills to effectively handle social situations
- help you practice questioning and reframing worried ideas provide advice on how to manage anxiety in a productive way

Chapter Seven

PUBLIC SPEAKING AND SOCIAL ANXIETY

P ublic speaking anxiety is extremely common; in fact, many people fear it more than death! The sensation varies from person to person, ranging from mild anxiety to severe panic or paralysis.

Those who suffer from social anxiety disorder are more likely to be afraid of public speaking (SAD). Regardless of whether we're giving a formal presentation to an audience or asking for a raise from our employer, speaking in front of a group is a crucial ability to master.

It is possible to overcome these worries and give a more confident speech, as intimidating as it may appear. It will take some effort and practice to break old patterns, but it is feasible. Few, if any, people are born experts when it comes to public speaking. It, like so many other duties in our personal and professional life, is a taught skill.

Consider public speaking as a skill you can learn, rather than an innate ability you were born with or without. If you change your mind about public speaking and follow the procedures outlined below, you, like anyone else, will be able to speak publicly with ease.

SAD and speech anxiety

Public speaking anxiety is a type of social anxiety disorder that is also known as speech anxiety or performance anxiety (SAD). One of the most common types of mental health issues is social anxiety disorder, commonly known as social phobia.

Symptoms

The symptoms of public speaking anxiety are similar to those of social anxiety disorder, except they only occur when speaking in front of an audience.

If you suffer from public speaking anxiety, you may be concerned weeks or months before a speech or presentation, and you are likely to experience severe physical symptoms of anxiety during the speech, such as:

- shaking
- blushing
- heart-pounding
- trembling voice
- breathing problems
- dizziness
- stomach ache

Causes

The fight or flight response—a rush of adrenaline that prepares you for danger—causes these symptoms. It's easy to feel as if you've lost control of your body when there's no genuine danger. This makes it difficult to perform well in public and may cause you to avoid situations where you will have to talk in front of others.

Diagnosis

If public speaking anxiety has a substantial impact on your life, it may be classified as SAD. This fear of public speaking anxiety can lead to a variety of issues, including:

- Changing college courses to avoid having to give an oral presentation
- Changing careers or occupations
- Refusing promotions due to public speaking commitments
- Failure to deliver a speech when it is required (e.g., best man at a wedding)

You may have SAD if you experience severe anxiety when speaking in public, and it interferes with your ability to live your life as you like.

Anxiety management

Effective remedies for public speaking anxiety are, fortunately, available. Medication, therapy, or a mix of the two may be used in such a treatment.

Therapy

Short-term therapy, such as systematic desensitization and cognitive-behavioral therapy (CBT), can help people learn how to cope with anxiety symptoms and the anxious thoughts that cause them.

Request a referral from your doctor to a therapist specializing in this type of therapy; it will be especially beneficial if the therapist has experience with social anxiety and/or public speaking anxiety.

Virtual reality (VR) therapy has also been an effective approach to addressing public speaking anxiety in studies. According to one study, students treated with virtual reality therapy had favorable results as short as a week after only one to twelve sessions. According to the study, VR sessions were also found to be helpful while being less invasive than in-person treatment sessions.

Medication

Ask your doctor about medication that can assist if you suffer from public speaking anxiety that gives you substantial distress. Short-term drugs known as beta-blockers (e.g., propranolol) can be taken to prevent anxiety symptoms before a speech or presentation.

Other drugs, like as selective serotonin reuptake inhibitors (SSRIs) and serotonin-norepinephrine reuptake inhibitors, may be recommended for the long-term therapy of SAD (SNRIs). When combined with treatment, you may find that the medicine helps you overcome your fear of public speaking.

How to get ready for a talk

There are a variety of tactics you can employ to manage speech anxiety and improve your public speaking skills in general, in addition to traditional treatment. Better preparation implies better performance when it comes to public speaking. Better preparation will increase your confidence and make it easier for you to focus on delivering your message.

Even if you have SAD, you may produce a successful speech or presentation with the right therapy and preparation time.

Preparation for a speech

Taking some time to prepare before giving a speech will help you control your anxiety. Before giving a speech or performing in front of an audience, make the following preparations:

• Select a topic that piques your curiosity. Choose a topic that you are passionate about if you have the opportunity. If you are unable to select a topic, consider taking an approach to a topic that interests you. As an example, as an introduction to your speech, you could present a personal anecdote that relates to the topic. This will keep you interested in your subject and driven to research and prepare for it. Others will sense your energy and be interested in what you have to say when you present.

• Familiarize yourself with the location. Before giving your speech, go to the conference room, classroom, auditorium, or banquet hall where you'll be giving it. If at all feasible, attempt to practice at least once in the setting where you will be speaking. Knowing your way around the venue and where the necessary audio-visual components are ahead of time will give you one less thing to worry about during your speech.

• Make a request for accommodations. Changes to your work environment that assist you in managing your anxiety are known as accommodations. This could include requesting a platform, having a pitcher of ice water on hand, bringing in audiovisual equipment, or even staying seated if necessary. You may be qualified for them under the Americans with Disabilities Act if you have been diagnosed with an anxiety disorder such as social anxiety disorder (SAD) (ADA).

It's not a scripted situation. Have you ever sat through a speech when the speaker read word for word from a prepared script? Most likely, you don't remember much of what was said. Instead, make a list of crucial topics that you may return to on paper or notecards.

Make a schedule for yourself. Make a plan for dealing with nervousness on the day before a speech or presentation. This exercise should assist you in getting into the right frame of mind and maintaining a relaxed condition. Exercising or practicing meditation the morning of a speech is an example.

Tips for improving public speaking skills

Visualization and practice

Even people who are used to speaking in public rehearse their speeches several times to ensure that they are perfect. You can gain confidence in your abilities to deliver your speech by practicing it 10, 20, or even 30 times.

If your talk has a time constraint, timing yourself during practice runs and make any necessary adjustments to your topic to fit within the allotted time. Getting a lot of practice will help you gain confidence.

Prepare yourself for tough inquiries

Try to anticipate difficult questions and critical comments that can come before giving your presentation, and prepare responses ahead of time. Deal with a problematic audience member by complimenting them or finding something on which you can both agree.

"Thank you for your essential inquiry," or "I greatly appreciate your comment," for example. Demonstrate that you are open-minded and unconcerned. Say you'll look into it if you don't know how to answer the question.

Get some perspective on things

Speak in front of a mirror or record yourself on a smartphone during a practice run. Make a mental note of how you appear and any nervous tendencies you should avoid. This stage is best completed after you've received anxiety treatment, such as therapy or medication.

Consider yourself as a winner

Did you know that your brain can't detect the difference between a genuine and an imagined activity? That is why professional athletes employ visualization to help them improve their athletic performance. Imagine yourself wowing the audience with your fantastic oratorical talents while you practice your speech (remember 10, 20, or even 30 times!). What you imagine will eventually convert into what you're capable of.

Accept a certain amount of anxiousness

Even professional performers feel nervous excitement before a performance; in fact, most people believe that a little nervousness helps you speak more effectively. Accept that you will always be nervous about giving a speech, but that this is natural and expected.

Setting objectives

Make it a personal goal to become an exceptional public speaker rather than merely getting by. You may improve your public speaking skills with the right treatment and a lot of practice. It's possible that you'll appreciate it!

Put things into context. If public speaking isn't one of your strong suits, keep in mind that it's only one facet of your personality. We all have distinct areas where we excel. Instead, make it a goal to become more at ease in front of an audience so that public speaking fear doesn't get in the way of your other life goals.

Chapter Eight

SIMPLE STEPS TO FEELING MORE SOCIALLY CONFIDENT

Many people may be suffering in quiet since social anxiety disorder is frequently misunderstood. It's about a lot more than being shy and unwilling to speak up in large groups. It can completely control and obstruct your daily existence.

Young people suffering from social anxiety

Simple duties can become nearly impossible to accomplish if you suffer from social anxiety and fear of social interactions. According to the Anxiety and Depression Association of America, some 15 million adults in the United States suffer from social anxiety, with young teens transitioning to secondary school or college being particularly vulnerable. Symptoms of social anxiety disorder are said to start around the age of thirteen.

The good news is that you can learn new habits to help you cope with and conquer your social anxiety.

Confront your nervous and negative thoughts

It may appear like there is little you can do about how you feel or think at times. However, there are a number of things that can assist.

Reducing the symptoms of social anxiety can be as simple as challenging your mentality and negative ideas. Begin by noticing the worried thoughts that spontaneously arise when you consider social situations.

After that, examine and challenge these ideas. Examine why you think this way and whether your first reaction is truly reflective of how you feel or if you're simply presuming the worst. Changing your way of thinking is a long process with no quick fixes, but the mind is a strong tool, and it is doable.

Be aware of your surroundings

Mindfulness and mindful meditation allow you to be present and aware of your thoughts and feelings non-judgmental and positive. Researchers discovered that meditation influenced activity in specific parts of the brain in a study published in the journal Social Cognitive and Affective Neuroscience.

Four 20-minute mindfulness meditation workshops were held for participants with normal levels of anxiety. They discovered that mindfulness training reduced anxiety levels by up to 39%.

Go to a coffee shop

Take your tablet or laptop to your local coffee shop if you prefer viewing movies online or catching up on your favorite TV show. Do something you enjoy and are at ease with in a setting that would normally make you nervous.

You'll be pushing your boundaries while maintaining the familiarity and comfort of being able to focus solely on what you're doing. Hopefully, you'll be able to challenge yourself while remaining in your emotional comfort zone.

Create a hierarchy of exposure

Identify and rate the level of anxiety you experience in each social situation. For example, a score of 0 indicates no anxiety while a score of 10 indicates a full-fledged panic episode.

Make a note of how you think you would react in each event, no matter how minor or major. From asking a stranger on the tube for the time to strolling into a room at a gathering. It's crucial to write down your predictions on a piece of paper so that when the time comes to experience it, you'll know how you expected to feel.

Don't put all of your attention on yourself

When you're in a circumstance that makes you feel extremely uncomfortable, it's difficult to stop the constant mental chatter. We frequently focus inward, on ourselves and how others will see us, nearly usually presuming a negative outcome. The fear that when you enter into a room, everyone will be staring at you and criticizing you in some way? This isn't correct.

Stop worrying about yourself and what others think of you. Concentrate on the people around you, strive to be present, and form true connections. Because no one is perfect, strive to stay in the moment and pay attention to what is being said.

Adopt a better lifestyle

The mind and body are inextricably intertwined, and how you manage your body has a huge impact on the rest of your life, including your anxiety levels. Small modifications in your lifestyle can help you gain self-confidence and manage better with anxiety symptoms.

You can avoid or limit your caffeine intake by not drinking coffee or caffeinated drinks after a specific hour. Energy drinks are stimulants, which can make anxiety symptoms worse.

Make physical activity a priority in your day and aim to be active at least once a day; even a quick walk during your lunch break is a good way to get it in.

Alcohol should only be consumed in moderation; while it may seem to relax your nerves, it might actually increase your chances of having an anxiety attack. Stay hydrated by drinking plenty of water and getting enough good sleep. When you don't get enough sleep, you're more prone to anxiety, and your mood suffers as a result.

According to new research, sleep deprivation can actually induce anxiety disorders.

Take a deep breath in and out

Increased heart rate, pounding chest, dizziness, and muscle strain are among physical indicators of anxiety. Taking a minute to stop and slow your breath can help you regain control of your body.

Simply sit down, relax, and take the deepest breath you've taken all day and hold it for four seconds. Then slowly exhale, expelling out as much air as you can. Take another deep inhale, this time filling your stomach with air, and repeat until your breathing returns to normal.

Be assured in your actions

Adults who suffer from social phobia and severe shyness are in the majority. In the same way, you learned to ride a bike, and you may learn to be confident. People will positively respond if you act more confidently.

This does not imply that you must be the class clown or the focus of attention at all times. It's simply a matter of becoming pushier, and something that is frightening at first will become less so over time.

Seek out social situations and participate in them

Make a concerted effort to interact with others. Seek out helpful social surroundings to assist you in overcoming your concerns. Starting with a social skills training class could be a good place to start. Before venturing out into the real world, you may perfect your social interactions here. This will teach you what to say and do when you're in a social scenario that you're not comfortable with or are nervous about.

Take care of yourself

Nobody is flawless, and everyone has experienced embarrassment at some point in their lives. It's not easy to overcome social anxiety, and there will be instances when you think negatively and revert to old patterns.

If you're exhausted or run down, you can feel more apprehensive than usual, but it doesn't indicate you've failed. Simply take a moment to breathe deeply, focus on the present moment, and practice the strategies you've been learning.

Have a conversation

Ideally, you will begin to feel more secure during talks once you have overcome your social anxiety and shyness. Talking to someone can be difficult, and knowing what to say can be even more difficult. An uneasy silence can feel like it lasts a lifetime at times. Talking to people one at a time will help you become less apprehensive.

Be brave and face your fears

Face your anxieties as the ultimate step. If you don't expose yourself to situations that make you uneasy, you'll never be able to overcome social anxiety. You won't be assisting yourself or supporting personal progress if you use avoidance as a coping mechanism.

Exposure therapy, or addressing your anxieties, has been demonstrated in numerous trials to be useful in treating anxiety disorders. However, research suggests that exposure should be done with caution. As a result, start with a social engagement or activity that only marginally increases your anxiety and gradually increase it.

It takes time for new neural pathways for social interactions to emerge, therefore overcoming social anxiety is a long process.

Is your social anxiety interfering with your day-to-day activities? Then don't be afraid to seek expert assistance in whichever manner you're most comfortable with. These are excellent methods for overcoming social anxiety.

Despite the fact that it appears to be an insurmountable challenge, it is well worth overcoming so that you can live your life to the fullest.

Chapter Nine

SELF CONFIDENCE

Self-confidence is a mindset about one's own strengths and skills. It implies that you accept and trust yourself and that you are in command of your life. You have a good outlook on yourself and are aware of your talents and weaknesses. You speak assertively, set realistic expectations and goals, and can handle criticism.

On the other side, low self-confidence might make you feel insecure, make you meek or submissive, and make it difficult to trust people. You might feel unwanted, inferior, or sensitive to criticism.

Whether or not you are self-assured depends on the situation. For example, you may be confident in some areas, such as academics, but not in others, such as relationships.

All about self-confidence

Having high or poor self-confidence is primarily based on your views rather than your real ability. Perceptions are how you think about yourself, and they might be inaccurate.

Low self-confidence can be caused by various events, such as growing up in a judgmental and unsupportive environment, being separated from friends or family for the first time, evaluating yourself too harshly, or being terrified of failure. People with poor self-esteem frequently make logical blunders.

How do you raise a confident son?

Boys are still expected to be rugged, strong, and stoic, according to societal standards. Denying feelings and vulnerability, on the other hand, can be damaging. Boys may be confident and successful if their feelings are validated, they are taught to channel their anger into healthy outlets, and they are encouraged to seek help when they need it.

Why is self confidence so important?

Learning how to gain confidence is beneficial in many aspects of your life, but it is especially critical during times when you feel like giving up. Being confident is non-negotiable if you are a leader in a position that requires you to be convincing and trustworthy. No one wants to follow a leader who appears insecure. Lack of confidence can significantly impact your ability to assemble a winning team and lead them to achieve your common objectives.

Even if you're not a leader, confidence is essential for working as part of a team in a variety of settings - whether you're in sales or need to maintain a confident demeanor throughout frequent customer interactions. Being self-assured allows you to develop fast connections and form relationships that will benefit both you and your organization.

It's also crucial to know how to be self-assured outside of the office. Learning how to be more self-assured can help you find a partner with whom you can form a healthy relationship. It can also help you deal with disagreement successfully and seek out new changes that will help you grow as a person.

The principles of self-confidence

You must be willing to modify your state if you want to learn how to be more confident. At any given time of day, your condition is essentially your mood, and how you feel about yourself at the time has an impact on your mood.

The good news is that, as long as you know-how, you can change your state at any time, regardless of what's going on around you. Here are three confidence principles that everybody can benefit from and some real-life examples to help you use them in any situation.

Body language

Do you want to learn how to be more self-assured? Just act the part! Physiology is crucial when it comes to learning how to be confident, and mastering the body language of confidence may put you on the road to success. Consider someone you know who you regard as incredibly self-assured. You undoubtedly sensed their confidence before they even started speaking when you first met them.

Because of the way they held themselves and moved, you could tell they were confident. They looked you in the eyes, shook your hand firmly, and stood tall.

Now do a brief inventory of your physical condition.

What is the state of your posture? What is your breathing pattern? Slouching, shallow breathing, and hanging your head are all signs of being in a bad mood. Controlling how your body moves and how you portray yourself gives you the power to influence how you feel.

Positivity

Positive thinking can present itself in a variety of ways. Change your concentration first because energy flows where it is focused. Rather than focusing on all of the ways something could go wrong, consider all of the ways it could go right.

Consider how you'll deliver your presentation and how thrilled your colleagues will be to hear it. What you focus on, including what you focus on within your own head, becomes your reality. Change your negative words to positive ones and begin to see the sunny side of things. You can change your state by altering your emphasis, both inside and outward. You can transform your life by changing your state.

A perspective of growth

What do you believe it takes to be self-assured? You might believe that confidence comes only after a lot of success – that you can only learn to be confident in yourself once you've made a lot of money. This type of basic conviction significantly restricts your options.

Confidence doesn't come from your accomplishments on the outside; it comes from within. If you're confident, you'll be able to pick yourself up and try again rather than throwing in the towel if you fail. Your beliefs will eventually solidify after you begin taking practical activities toward your goal of becoming confident.

It's time to embrace a growth mentality and believe that you can learn to be more self-assured.

Common questions about self-confidence

Confidence isn't something you're born with. It is a skill that can be learned and honed over time.

Practice in social situations can help you gain social confidence. Individuals can watch the structure and flow of any conversation before participating, and they can prepare questions or subjects to discuss in advance.

When people are tormented by self-doubt, anxiety can set in, therefore putting oneself in and becoming accustomed to the circumstance they fear might reassure them that nothing genuinely horrible will happen. With practice, the action becomes easier.

Personal and professional accomplishments can provide a sense of confidence outside of a social situation. Setting and achieving goals might help people believe they are competent and capable.

How can I boost my self-esteem on a daily basis?

Being self-assured is understanding that you can deal with the emotional consequences of whatever situation you find yourself in. Begin by acknowledging all feelings, even the ones that are challenging, rather than avoiding them. Speaking up for yourself, limiting self-criticism, and other methods can all aid in the development of emotional strength and confidence.

How do I get confidence in a particular field?

Confidence isn't a one-size-fits-all concept: you can be confident in some areas while lacking confidence in others. Observe others, practice yourself, and seek advice from experts to polish your skills and create self-efficacy in whatever new topic you pick.

How can I improve my mental toughness?

Mental toughness can aid in the development of confidence by allowing you to overcome hurdles. Set goals, change your mindset from negative to realistic, challenge yourself every day, and learn to handle discomfort. These and other suggestions can aid in the gradual development of mental strength.

How can I boost my confidence in preparation for a job interview?

When others are judging you, it's natural to feel scared or insecure—especially in a high-stakes situation. The basis of a successful interview is built on doing study ahead of time and exhibiting conscientiousness, meditating on your flaws so you can communicate how you've learned from them, and being kind, complimentary, and self-assured.

Overconfidence and underconfidence

People who have a realistic assessment of their talents might achieve a healthy balance between too little and too much confidence. In school, in business, or in social situations, a lack of confidence can inhibit people from taking chances and embracing possibilities.

Too much self-assurance can come across as arrogance, cockiness, or narcissism. Overestimating one's talents can lead to issues such as not finishing jobs on time.

What's the difference between narcissism and confidence?

Insecurities and defense mechanisms can lead to narcissism, whereas self-awareness and the ability to tolerate and reflect on one's insecurities lead to confidence. Narcissism encompasses a sense of superiority over others, whereas confidence instills a personal sense of being capable and competent.

Why are narcissists so appealing to us?

According to one recent study, individuals prefer those who are higher in narcissism over those who are lower in narcissism, which could be because people underestimate how much self-esteem narcissists have. The ability to project a strong sense of self-assurance that puts others at ease could be the key to narcissists' attraction.

What are the causes of someone's lack of self-assurance?

Genetics, temperament, cultural background, and early life experiences such as parental style or past trauma are just a few factors that influence a person's confidence level. Although we have little control over those factors, there are still many strategies to acquire confidence throughout our life.

What are the consequences of a lack of confidence?

People with low self-esteem may be hesitant to pursue new chances, such as a career change or a new personal relationship, for fear of failure or embarrassment. By considering whether opportunities are viable and the spectrum of possible outcomes, people can ensure that their lack of confidence prevents them from succeeding.

How to raise confident kids

As they negotiate academics, friendships, and sexual relationships, children—particularly adolescents—can experience uneasiness and self-doubt. On the other hand, parents may help their children develop self-confidence by giving them the tools they need.

How do you raise confident kids?

Although parents may be tempted to assist their children with every difficulty that arises, standing aside and allowing children to solve problems on their own can help develop executive function abilities, motivate them, and establish a strong sense of self-agency and confidence.

How do you raise a confident adolescent?

Parents can help their children develop self-confidence by supporting their goals, treating mistakes as learning opportunities and failure as proof of trying, encouraging practice and tenacity, and not projecting their fears onto their children. These and other answers can assist teenagers in developing self-confidence.

How do you bring up a confident daughter?

Recognize, consider, and trust your daughter's emotions. She will learn to trust her emotions by empathizing with them and empathizing with them. She will trust who she is if she trusts how she feels. Instead of lashing out, she will be able to express how she feels and work through problems.

How to be more confident

What are the similarities and differences between such principles? It's all about learning to control your emotions, and you must shift your perspective and thinking and make the decision to be confident. That can be easier said than done at times, but there are concrete steps you can take to help you apply these ideas to your confidence.

Get rid of limiting beliefs

To actually learn how to be self-assured, you must first learn to love yourself. You'll have confidence no matter what occurs in life if you practice self-love since that confidence will emanate from within.

On the other hand, many people never learn how to love themselves and instead acquire a lack of confidence early in life. They unknowingly develop restrictive attitudes about their own abilities and the types of relationships they deserve.

This leads to self-sabotage and the reinforcement of negative beliefs, which must be overcome before ultimate confidence can be achieved.

Decide what is important to you

Just as changing your body language can help you feel more confident when you aren't, sticking up for yourself when you don't think you deserve it can do the same.

Confident people may earn more money at work for one simple reason: they take credit for their accomplishments and do it when it counts. It's not bragging to tell your manager or CEO about a contribution you made that helped the organization achieve a goal or resulted in a beneficial outcome. It will not only make you appear good, but it will also make you feel good if you say it matter-of-factly.

Determine your primary human need

Determining what motivates your decisions is another crucial step in learning how to be confident in yourself. Certainty, importance, diversity, love/connection, growth, and contribution are the six human needs that we all share.

One of these requirements is more important to us than the others, and it influences every decision we make in life. It can even have an impact on our self-assurance. If assurance is your primary desire, you may feel uneasy in new situations. If your primary desire is significant, you'll begin to feel insecure if you don't receive it.

Improve your self conversation

Our words create our emotions, and our feelings create our world. Because of the stories we tell ourselves – and the words we use to tell them – we don't feel secure.

How do you converse with yourself in your head? Your inner monologue, often known as self-talk, has a significant impact on your confidence. When you catch yourself thinking poorly about your physique, replace it with a positive idea about yourself.

Use gratitude in your day-to-day life

Gratitude is essential to living a good life. Fear fades away and abundance arises when you are appreciative. Stop thinking of your body as something to look at – or, worse, something to look at for others. Your body isn't just a vessel or a work of art to be appreciated.

Consider all the things your body accomplishes for you. It will begin to feel more like a gift than a burden when you take a moment to appreciate all the things your body allows you to perform.

Change your psychological conditions

The quickest way to gain confidence is to drastically alter your physique. Straighten your back. Your shoulders should be squared, and your chest should be open. Take a deep breath. When walking, keep your strides short and purposeful to cover more territory. Maintaining this position helps you feel stronger, and your mind follows your body wherever it goes. You can also study the physiology of others to learn more about them and acquire a competitive advantage in negotiations. Certain indicators, like a person's body angle and the amount of physical space they occupy, can reveal how they view a situation – and how easily they can be persuaded.

Use power poses in practice

Connecting to your inner power is one of the most powerful methods to boost your confidence. We all have the strength within us, but it might be tough to remember that when we're feeling down.

To reconnect to your strong core, consider constructing your own particular power posture and inhaling deeply. Standing with your hands on your hips and feet shoulder-width apart, or standing with your head held high and your back straight, can be a yoga posture - warrior is particularly empowering – or standing with your head held high and your back straight. What matters is that your position accomplishes the objectives of waking your inner strength and carrying that strength and confidence into every contact.

Consider past successes

Just as changing your body language can help you feel more confident when you aren't, sticking up for yourself when you don't think you deserve it can do the same.

Confident people may earn more money at work for one simple reason: they take credit for their accomplishments and do it when it counts. It's not bragging to tell your manager or CEO about a contribution you made that helped the organization achieve a goal or resulted in a beneficial outcome. It will not only make you appear good, but it will also make you feel good if you say it in a matter-of-fact manner.

Even the most self-assured among us have a long list of accomplishments. Imagine a recent accomplishment or a period when you successfully handled a comparable issue if you're scared or confused about a future situation.

You may have never given a company-wide presentation, but you've confidently delivered presentations to clients over the phone. Those who wish to learn how to be more confident frequently forget that they've had plenty of opportunities to do so in the past, and reliving these experiences might help them realize their full potential.

Visualize your goals

Positive visualization is a useful strategy to use on the path to learning how to gain confidence. When you repeatedly envision something, your mind comes to believe that it has actually occurred.

When the time comes to make that presentation, ask for a raise, or confront a coworker, your brain believes to yourself, "I got this." That is self-assurance. Consider a specific job circumstance. Consider yourself successful, and try to avoid any thoughts of failure. Keep in mind that you get what you concentrate on.

Make eye contact

Making eye contact can be unpleasant at first for individuals who aren't sure how to be confident. However, just like changing your physiology, you must take action in order to gain confidence.

Connecting with individuals and displaying confidence through eye contact is one of the most effective ways to radiate confidence when meeting new people and can help to develop long-term relationships. To avoid appearing excessively serious or making the other person uncomfortable, follow the 80/20 rule of meeting someone's eyes 80 percent of the time and focusing on something else the other 20%.

Live in the moment

One of the most difficult aspects of partnerships is gaining confidence. It can be difficult to forgive and let go of the past if you've been wronged in a previous relationship - or in your present one. We want to avoid pain and satisfy our desire for certainty, yet doing so keeps us from living in the moment.

Learn to be grateful for what you have right now, rather than fretting about what will happen tomorrow or yesterday. Allow your thoughts to wander, be present at the moment, and confidence will follow.

Chapter Ten

HOW TO BE MORE SECURE WITH YOURSELF

Insecurity affects a large number of people. Whether you're contemplating a big decision or just want to boost your confidence, overcoming insecurity is a crucial first step. The good news is that you can start moving in the correct direction and overcome your insecurity right now.

You've probably met a lot of insecure folks. Most of the time, it's a silent battle. Everyone suffers from a lack of self-confidence from time to time. However, if your inability to feel safe is causing you significant stress, you must take action. Self-doubt, if left uncontrolled, can prevent you from achieving your goals, generate interpersonal strain, and lead to harmful coping techniques.

When it comes to self-doubt, where does it come from? And why do so many people struggle to feel safe in their own skin?

According to one theory, insecurities are established from childhood when people are exposed to negativity, whether it is directed at them or they watch caretakers expressing negative beliefs about themselves. Insecurities from childhood can remain into adulthood, causing issues with self-esteem and mental health.

Developing emotional security

Make an effort to be mindful

Mindfulness is the practice of noticing your thoughts and feelings in the present moment to create an active awareness of yourself and your environment. According to research, practicing mindfulness can help you feel more confident in yourself and your interactions with others, leading to greater overall contentment over time.

Make an effort to breathe slowly and deliberately.

Slowly inhale for five seconds while counting to five, hold your breath for five seconds, then slowly exhale for five seconds.

Keep your attention on the present moment.

Return your focus to how your body feels and the sensory information around you whenever your mind wanders.

Mindfulness requires a lot of practice and patience to master. Working at it every day will make you feel happier, more secure, and at ease over time.

<u>Make an effort to connect with others</u>

Seeking emotional support from individuals you care about and trust can give you a fantastic sense of safety. To re-establish that connection in your life, try making up with a buddy with whom you've had a falling out, or practice asking for help/advice from those closest to you.

Reaching out to friends and rekindling old friendships might help you remember that you have people who love and care about you.

A heart-to-heart chat with someone you care about can help you build your bond with them. Make sure to tell your friend/partner/family member how much you love and support them, and ask them to do the same for you.

Satisfy your emotional needs

We all have emotional needs that we try to meet through romantic relationships, friendships, and family ties. Each link provides a unique level of comfort, security, and acceptance. If you're feeling uncertain emotionally, it's possible that one or more of your key relationships aren't providing your emotional demands.

Examine your personal connections honestly. In those partnerships, do you ever feel unloved or uncared for? Do you ever feel safe around other people, or do you always feel a little insecure?

If you believe one of your relationships is making you feel insecure, try talking to that friend/lover/family member about how you're feeling. Decide what that person could do better, then have an open, loving conversation about your needs and how they may be addressed better.

Learn to put your faith in others

Many people experience emotional insecurity as a result of a lack of trust. This could be due to failed previous relationships or friendships, or it could just be a deep-seated fear of abandonment. Whatever your cause for mistrust, you must understand that you cannot live a life without trusting others. Just because something has gone wrong in the past (or even several times), doesn't mean it will happen again.

Consider whether your lack of confidence in others arises from a lack of faith in yourself. Many people unwittingly project their anxieties and negative feelings onto others. Is it possible that you have doubts about your relationship because you have doubts about yourself?

Often, your mistrust of another person stems from a lack of faith in your own ability to make sound decisions. You must determine whether you are prepared to incur the risk of being injured if you want to be friends or lovers with someone. Believe in yourself and trust that if a circumstance like this comes, you'll know what to do.

Having a secure sense of self

Stop putting yourself in comparison to others

Comparing yourself to others is one of the most harmful things you can do to your self-esteem. This is especially true when it comes to physical comparisons, such as comparing your body to stars, actresses, and models in the media. Intellectual comparisons, artistic comparisons, and career comparisons are all examples of this.

Discover your own style and beauty. You're a one-of-a-kind and lovely person, and comparing your life/body/career to others does you a disservice.

Always keep in mind that you are ultimately responsible for your own pleasure and that personal fulfillment and self-love must originate from inside. Be gentle with yourself and try to respect yourself for who you are now, rather than who you want to be in the future.

Recognize and change negative core beliefs

Everyone has a set of essential beliefs that define who we are in relation to the rest of the world. Many of these essential ideas emerge early in childhood, but others emerge later in life (or can be altered). Unpleasant core beliefs are formed by negative life events, distorted/irrational expectations, and negative self-evaluation.

Examine whether your life experiences have to lead you to assume there is something "wrong" with you, and then reconsider what you consider "normal."

Can you connect any unfavorable self-perceptions you have to a specific person, place, or event? If that's the case, why do you believe that idea is an absolute truth based on a single person's viewpoint or the occurrence of a single unpleasant event?

"Would I ever say the things I think about myself to someone else about their body, work, or lifestyle choices?" ask yourself honestly. Why say something nasty to yourself if you wouldn't say it to others?

Examine the proof of your unfavorable self-perceptions. What are those beliefs based on, and has there ever been anything great that has come from holding on to those views?

Create new possibilities for you to have safe, healthy, and positive experiences that you haven't had before. Instead of abandoning your goals, approach situations you've previously avoided (as long as they're safe) and see challenges through to the end.

Make time for yourself to do safe, enjoyable things, and make you feel good about yourself.

Make an effort to be more aggressive with the people you care about. Don't be bossy, but make sure your voice and ideas are heard.

Recognize and appreciate your abilities

It's easy to lose sight of how talented, strong, and interesting you are as a person during daily life's stress. It's probably even more difficult to remember your strengths if you have low self-esteem. Take a few minutes each day to exercise self-awareness of your personal strengths, and keep a notebook to track how your self-esteem improves as you devote more time to self-appreciation.

Make a list of your skills and abilities. Make a new list of your accomplishments. Make a third list of qualities/characteristics you admire in others and recognize in yourself (to varying degrees). Read through these lists on a regular basis, and make a fresh set every few weeks. Keep your old lists and compare them to see if anything has changed after a few months.

Make a written list of your best qualities with the help of a close friend, family member, or love partner. Request that they write about why they care about you, what distinguishes you from others, and what you do better than anybody else. Keep this list with you at all times (maybe in your wallet or purse) and refer to it whenever you are feeling down about yourself.

Don't forget to look after yourself

If you're insecure about yourself, it's possible that you haven't given yourself enough attention recently. Everyone has emotional and physical needs, and when those needs aren't addressed, we feel awful. Take care of yourself on a daily basis, and you'll most likely feel much better in your skin.

Spend some time on your personal hygiene every day. Brush and floss your teeth twice a day, shower or bathe, style your hair, shave, and trim your nails on a daily basis.

Consume a nutritious, well-balanced diet. Avoid junk food and make sure you're receiving enough vitamins and nutrients.

Increase your physical activity. Find ways to get some exercise every day, such as walking or riding your bike instead of driving to run errands. Aim for a more vigorous cardio routine three times each week in addition to your daily walking or cycling.

Dress in clothes that make you feel confident in your own skin. Figure out what makes you feel most comfortable and confident, whether it's narrow, form-fitting clothes or baggier, looser clothes, and wear those confidence clothes as much as possible.

Make certain you get enough rest. Most adults require between seven and nine hours of sleep per night, depending on their age.

Create SMART objectives

Getting your goals accomplished is a great approach to feel more secure and confident in yourself. Many people become distressed when they are unable to reach their objectives; but, rather than beating yourself up, assess whether your objectives are attainable or even measurable. Experts agree that setting S.M.A.R.T. (Specific, Measurable, Achievable, Results-focused, and Time-bound) goals will help you set meaningful goals that give you a sense of purpose and success.

Be specific - exactly define what you intend to do straightforwardly and simply.

Measurable - Set goals that can be measured in some way. If you don't have a mechanism to track your progress, you'll never know if you're making meaningful progress toward your objective.

Achievable - your objectives should stretch you a little, but they should ultimately be something you can achieve.

Results-oriented - your outcomes rather than your actions should measure your development. Don't just work toward your objective to see how far you've come. Measure your progress by how far you've come toward achieving your final goal. Take pride in the "little" successes you've had along the way.

Time-bound – set a realistic deadline for yourself. Don't expect to see results right away, but don't wait a year to start putting in some effort. Decide on a reasonable, realistic timetable for completion and stick to it.

Forgive yourself and others

If you've spent any time on this planet, chances are you've hurt someone or been hurt by someone else. These offenses may have been intentional or unintentional, but many individuals have a hard time forgetting about them. Playing a scenario you regret over and over in your head, on the other hand, will never undo what you've done. It will only cause you to suffer and make you feel bad about yourself and others.

Keep in mind that making mistakes allows you to learn from them. You may have caused or been caused harm to others, but the essential thing is that you learned from your mistakes, and those who have caused you to harm have also learned from their mistakes.

Instead of meditating on what you wish you'd done differently, consider what you'd like to do differently right now. Because the past cannot be changed and the future does not yet exist, the only time you can change is now.

Concentrate on how you can be the best version of yourself right now, and figure out how to make that vision a reality.

Look for something to be thankful for

Take some time each day to think about the people and events that have shaped your life into what it is now. Obviously, not everything/everyone has been fantastic all of the time, but chances are you've had some pretty amazing experiences and met a lot of inspiring, caring individuals in your life. Remember that you would not be who you are now if people had not shown you love, and you had not been born into the conditions you did.

Nobody's life is flawless all of the time. Many people, in fact, suffer their entire lives. Try to remember that no matter how bad your life is, there are those who have it worse, and those people undoubtedly admire your existence.

Count your blessings for those who have shown you love and taught you how to love. Consider how sad and lonely your life would be if it weren't for the affection you've received from others, at least at some point in your life.

Make an effort to appreciate the small pleasures in life. Every day, see the sunrise or set and be grateful that you've lived to see another day - many individuals can't say the same about the present.

Feeling financially secure

Define what you want to accomplish

To you, what does financial security entail? You may not have a realistic dream if it only implies being wealthy. If it means paying off your debts, investing in your children's college fund, or preparing for retirement, you have a realistic end goal to aim toward.

Having a clear understanding of why you want to save money might help you stay motivated and on track.

Once you've established a clear financial goal, a financial planner can assist you in determining the best ways to invest or save your money.

Examine your current situation

If you want to feel financially secure, you should first assess your existing financial status to see what, if anything, needs to be changed. Examining your money, including your savings and expenses, is the first step.

Keep track of your earnings as well as your savings (if any).

Keep track of your spending on a daily, weekly, and monthly basis. Keep a little notebook in your pocket or purse and record all of your expenses. This covers the items you purchase, the bills you pay, and the dates and hours when those expenses occurred. You should also keep track of how you felt at the time of any transactions.

Do you have a habit of buying stuff for yourself when you're upset or stressed? Are there any purchases you've purchased on the spur of the moment that you didn't really need or could have gotten for less elsewhere?

Check to see whether you're spending more than you're earning. This will quickly put you in debt, and it will be difficult to get out of debt after you've done so.

You don't have to deny yourself everything that makes you happy, but you need to set some limitations and boundaries. Don't go on shopping sprees just because you want to, and don't buy things you don't actually need.

Reduce your spending

Some costs, such as rent, utilities, and groceries, cannot be avoided. Even with these required expenses, you can save money by shopping wisely and eliminating unnecessary purchases.

Bring a shopping list with you whenever you go grocery shopping and stick to it.

Purchase things that are on sale, generic/off-brand, or in quantity wherever possible. This can save you a lot of money and provide you with the same vital goods at a much lower cost.

Whenever feasible, try to buy used items.

Compare prices before making a purchase. If you check through advertisements, online and in the newspaper, you're likely to find identical goods for a lesser price elsewhere.

Make your own meals at home. Bring a sack lunch and a thermos of coffee to work every day to avoid dining out as much as possible. This will allow you to save a significant amount of money, which you can put toward other costs or a savings account.

Look for low-cost or free entertainment. Many movies are available for free or at a cheap cost online (through legal streaming websites), or you can borrow books, CDs, and movies for free from the library.

When you're not at home, lower the temperature, and when you're sleeping, raise it. When you're at home and awake, try to use your heat or air conditioner the most. (However, if you have pets at home, keep in mind that they require a pleasant temperature at all times of the day and night, even if you are not around.)

Purchases should not be made on credit or with a credit card. You'll save a lot of worry (and debt) if you save up until you can afford your purchases.

Boost your earnings

Try acquiring a second part-time job or finding one full-time job if you're working part-time. Even if you're employed full-time, you can still find odd jobs to supplement your income. And if your current employment allows you to pay your bills, your side job can be devoted to your savings account!

Look in the classifieds or on job-listing websites for assistance.

Find simple side employment that doesn't conflict with your regular work schedule. You'll probably be able to discover advertisements for dog walkers, babysitters, or even part-time jobs.

Deposit into a savings account

It's fine if you have to save money for a while. For most people, it requires a lot of forethought and hard work, but the payoff of financial security is well worth it. Opening a savings account is an excellent method to get started saving. You can begin with a tiny amount, such as $20 per month or every paycheck. That weekly or monthly deposit adds up to significant savings over time.

Many financial institutions allow you to set up an automatic transfer, which automatically deposits a portion of your paycheck into your savings account.

Small debit/checking purchases are rounded up to the nearest dollar, and the change is put into your savings account in some banks' "Keep the Change" (or similar) programs. This is a simple and effective approach to saving money without even realizing it.

Unless it's a genuine emergency, try to avoid using your money. If you can wait until your next paycheck to make any expenditures, do so and keep your savings untouched.

CONCLUSION

S hyness is a personality attribute or emotional state marked by awkwardness, concern, or tension in the presence of others, particularly strangers. Although shyness is not a diagnosable mental health disease, someone who wants to overcome it may seek counseling.

Although someone with these disorders may also be shy, shyness is not synonymous with or associated with generalized anxiety, social anxiety, isolation, introversion, or agoraphobia.

Some people are embarrassed by their shyness or believe it is a bad personality attribute. Some even seek a "cure" to alleviate the uneasiness or tension they experience when interacting with others. It's important to remember that shyness is only one component of personality and that many other characteristics contribute to defining who a person is and how they interact with others.

Some people's shyness interferes with their daily lives to the point where they can't hold a conversation with others without bursting into tears or distancing themselves from the situation entirely. Shyness might make it difficult to completely enjoy hobbies, be productive at work, or maintain a fulfilling social life. For these reasons, a person may seek psychotherapy to assist them in dealing with their shyness or teach them how to cope and adjust to it when it occurs.

Shyness may be crippling, partly because shy people tend to avoid public situations and speak up and partly because they suffer from persistent worry.

If that describes you, rest assured that you are not alone: four out of ten people identify as shy.

The good news is that shyness can be overcome, and it is possible to break through with time, effort, and a desire to change.

You may need the support of a therapist or counselor if your shyness is severe, but most people can overcome it on their own.

This book has provided you with all the knowledge you need to overcome this psychological condition. We learned how to recognize shyness, distinguish it from social anxiety or simple introversion. We then analyzed in detail the path to take to overcome shyness through greater self-confidence and self-esteem. Now all that remains is to get to work and transform what we have learned into a new life, happier for us and for the people we love.

www.ingramcontent.com/pod-product-compliance
Lightning Source LLC
Chambersburg PA
CBHW071518080526
44588CB00011B/1471